Tradition
vs.
Traditionalism

The Apparent Heresy of Jesus?

by

Gerard A. Pisani Jr.

March 2016
(prior printing 2002)

Contents

Introduction

What is a heresy anyway? The dictionary says that it is an "opinion or doctrine at variance with the orthodox or accepted doctrine, especially of a church or religious system." According to the Gospel accounts, Jesus was, any number of times, at variance with the orthodox or accepted traditions of the leaders of his religious system. I suppose most of us, at least once in our lives, have questioned accepted doctrine. Perhaps we have even been at variance with our religious system.

The fear of being a heretic, however, may be the unrecognized source of a problem most people have in experiencing the fullness of life. John's Gospel speaks of the thief who comes only to steal, kill, and destroy, but continues by telling us that Jesus has come in order that we might have life—life in all its fullness!

In this book, I hope to share with you how I believe we all can experience an abundant life. I now recognize that the lack of such an experience may be due to our fear of heresy and an inappropriate use of tradition. That is why I wish to explore these issues with you, especially as they may be observed in the life of our Lord and the Church.

I have been a part of the Church all my life, although not always a part of the Episcopal Church, and I have always been bothered by something. Although I, for the most part, gained much strength and vitality from my relationship to Christ and the Church, deep within my heart I detected an uncomfortable feeling about a pervasive weakness and emptiness in most Christians. There was often something missing, but I was never able to point my finger to the source of the problem. In fact, it was not a topic that was easy to discuss with many people. Often I would be accused of lacking humility or of judging others when the topic arose.

The Church, which is really the people, was sometimes so alive and yet, more often than not, so dead. Promises were offered for abundant and eternal life, yet many Christian communities were barely making it or even in the process of dying. This scenario has been true, from my observance, in all the Christian traditions of which I have been a part.

I was raised in the Assemblies of God, where there always appeared to be excitement and progress. In fact, even to this day people in the Assemblies speak of themselves as the fastest growing denomination. With the lively music, awareness of spiritual gifts, celebration of healing, and the constant evangelical and revival atmosphere, one could easily agree that it was true. As a member of one of the faithful families in the Assemblies, however, I was also aware of the many Assembly churches in America where this was not so. My grandfather was a minister all his ordained life in places that were simply existing or dying. My uncle, who was also a minister in the Assemblies, only served in one congregation that was somewhat "alive." This realization saddened me by the age of twelve; it was one of the things that compelled me to move on. Unfortunately, I moved on with a sense of snobbery. With an air of self-righteousness I moved "up" to another evangelical tradition. In my teens and early adult life I wanted to be a part of a somewhat less "emotional" crowd and join with those who were more "intellectual." I assumed life was more actively present among those who celebrated and enjoyed knowledge and understanding. The services were more "dignified," and everyone was open to studying and learning. My new elders had the answers to life, and I was anxious to learn them and apply them. While there were popular and well-known Pentecostal evangelists, I was now traveling with the "real crowd," Billy Graham and Jack Wyrtzen, the international head of "Word of Life" fellowship! Jack was on hundreds of radio and television stations across the United States, with camps and conference centers in the Adirondacks, South America, and Mexico. I not only appeared on radio and television programs each week, I was privileged to travel all over as a part of these services and rallies in huge stadiums and auditoriums. In our travels, I was able to converse with and learn from many evangelists who were distinguished scholars and preachers.

While there were many outwardly large and successful places in this segment of the evangelical tradition, there were many more that were hardly making it. It likewise came to my attention that this branch of Christianity was not as great as I had originally expected. While primary in the United States, the Protestant tradition is not so well established in other countries. In spite of their enthusiastic support for many "foreign" missionaries, their popularity and forte was primarily in America. During my days in college, I was busy exploring many different sects within the Christian faith. Most of these were rather small, but 1 realized that smallness was not the problem. I still felt there was something lacking which I could not yet identify, but I came to realize it was not necessarily connected to size.

In my continuing quest, I moved on to the worldwide Anglican Communion. I assumed that this group of Christians possessed all one could ever wish for in church. Scholarship reigned high. Music and liturgy were superb! In many places around the world this elegance enhanced the mind, fed the soul, and warmed and stirred one's emotions with dignity and extravagance. While it was not the largest denomination in the United States, most of our presidents and many of our people in Congress were Episcopalians. This church brought people together from the four comers of our globe in some of the grandest historical structures imaginable. In fact, the largest cathedral in the world was the Episcopal cathedral in New York City— St. John the Divine. Even though I lived in one of the most vital and successful dioceses in this country, the Diocese of Newark, I was faced with a lack of life and vitality in many of the churches—especially in Hudson County. Here, in the midst of a rich and historic tradition, there were congregations who were discouraged, frustrated, and defeated. It was sad for me to recognize that there were still too many ailing and hurting congregations. Why were so many church and Christian people who spoke of the "good news" experiencing so much "bad news"?

As I look back on my many years and all the variety in my background, there is hardly a regret. I have actually come to love and appreciate most of what I have experienced. I realize how blessed and privileged I am to have acquired such a wide and varied heritage in the process. In fact, because of the openness of my present Episcopal tradition, I can appreciate the vitality added to my own life by these numerous experiences in my journey. I am truly grateful for the witness and influence of so many people in such diverse circumstances. But deep within my heart, I still recognized an uncomfortable feeling about something, yet I was unable to point my finger to the source of the problem.

Then, as I was preparing my sermon for Sunday, June 23, 1991, it suddenly dawned on me what may have been bothering me for those many years. As I studied the Scriptures in the lectionary appointed for that Sunday (Proper 7 of Year B in the Book of Common Prayer of the Episcopal Church, 1979), I saw something I had never noticed before. It quite possibly was the point that had been missing in my varied encounters with all parts of the Body of Christ. It was something that, for now, I will refer to as that Apparent Heresy of Jesus.

In the chapters of this book I will try to portray that which I now believe causes most religious and church problems. I hope to make this presentation in a practical and reasonable way. While I will attempt to present any facts in a trustworthy manner, this is not intended to be a scholarly work. I want everyone, the faithful and the lapsed, to seriously consider what I have to say. My hope is to bring an experience of perpetual and vital life to the whole Community of God.

Chapter 1

The Value of Tradition

Tradition is defined as "the handing down of statements, beliefs, leg- ends, customs, etc., from generation to generation...." Who of us would deny the importance of tradition? Where would we be without this legacy? Can we imagine being born into this world and having to start from scratch without any tradition? What an insurmountable task it would be without this inheritance we call tradition.

Most people seem to have little or no problem with tradition, but many of us recognize a problem with traditionalism. Traditionalism is defined as "adherence to tradition as authority, especially in matters of religion. A system of philosophy according to which ail knowledge of religious truth is derived from divine revelation and received by tra- ditional instruction."

The facility of knowledge from others, whether past or present, is an important foundation for our own understanding. Intelligent people thirst for this knowledge so as to build an adequate substructure for their own creativity. As we are stimulated and fed by others, we de- velop our own existential concepts that contribute to the traditions of our own generation. New ideas are born that broaden and enrich the concepts of our forebears, and life continues with fresh understanding for the new era.

I doubt that there would be very many—if any—who would deny the necessity and facility of tradition. Such a denial might be analo- gous to being against apple pie or motherhood. I can foresee only one problem others might have concerning traditions: there are so many! As our world grows smaller and we become more familiar with the wide assortment of cultures, we can become overwhelmed by the many resources from which we have to learn.

Traditionalism, however, has become a plague on our house. While there are significant minorities who are unfruitful in their lives for lack of root or tradition, there are many more who are being squelched or killed intellectually because of traditionalism. Those who insist, especially religious people, thwart many when there is only one way to act or think in life. This becomes especially twisted and life-threatening when humans propagate their "truth" with the claim of divine imprimatur.

I believe Jesus had this problem, too. The religious authorities of his day were not trying to share tradition, but rather, they were trying to impose their traditionalism on Jesus. It was in response to their imposition of traditionalism, not to the traditions, that Jesus reacted so vehemently. Each of the Gospel writers tells us several stories that bring this apparent struggle to the fore.

The most vivid story that comes to mind is the one in which Jesus "cleanses" the temple. It is recorded by all of the Gospel writers. Matthew sets the scene immediately in chapter twenty-one by saying, "Jesus went into the temple and drove out all those who were buying and selling there." He portrays Jesus as using Scriptures from Isaiah and Jeremiah when he refers to Jesus as saying, "It is written in the Scriptures that God said, 'My temple will be called a house of prayer. But you are making it a hideout for thieves!'" Matthew then quickly tells us about Jesus healing the blind and crippled who came to him in the temple as an object lesson to portray the true meaning and purpose of that holy place. Mark's Gospel, after setting a similar stage, immediately thickens the plot by having the religious leaders "looking for a way to kill Jesus." Luke agrees that they "wanted to kill him, but they could not find a way to do it, because all the people kept listening to him, not wanting to miss a single word." John is the one who dramatizes the way Jesus did it. John says, "So he made a whip from cords and drove all the animals out of the temple, both the sheep and the cattle; he overturned the tables of the moneychangers and scattered their coins; and he ordered the men who sold the pigeons, 'Take them out of here! Stop making my Father's house a marketplace!'" John also embellishes the latter part by having them challenge Jesus to demonstrate his authority by performing a miracle! Jesus responds by saying, "Tear down this temple, and in three days I will build it again." In response, the religious leaders question how he could do this, since it took forty years to build the temple in the first place. This, of course, was not the only confrontation Jesus had with the leadership of his day. It appears, at times, that Jesus was constantly and consistently questioned about his authority to do, or not to do, what they perceived the Law required. Some of the other stories that come to mind: Jesus healing a paralyzed man who was given access to Jesus through a hole in the roof (Mark 2:1-12). Jesus' visit to the home of a tax collector after he indicated he would like to become a follower (Mark 2:13-17). Jesus being questioned about his and his followers' failure to properly observe the laws of fasting (Mark 2:18-22). Jesus and his disciples picking wheat on the Sabbath because they were hungry (Mark 2:23-28). Jesus healing a man with a paralyzed hand on the Sabbath (Mark 3:1-6).

These stories and a host of others will attest to Jesus' dilemma in his apparent heresy regarding the religious laws and customs of his day. The way Jesus taught on many occasions will also support my point. As a prelude to many of his teachings in the beginning of Matthew's Gospel we hear a phrase such as, "You have heard that people were told in the past...But now I tell you..." This may demonstrate that Jesus was trying to make a distinction between tradition and traditionalism. It was not unusual to hear other statements from Jesus such as, "Do not think that I have come to do away with the Law of Moses and the teachings of the prophets." It was not only characteristic of Jesus to defend and explain these laws and teachings, he also was an example of one who had studied and treasured them. The continuation of the previous phrase that is attributed to Jesus might help emphasize my point, "Remember that as long as heaven and earth last, not the least point nor the smallest detail of the Law will be done away with" (Matt. 5:17-18).

There were also other occasions when Jesus tried to tell the people, especially those who were supporters of his ministry, to follow and keep the law. Jesus healed a man of a dreaded skin disease who knelt down and begged him for help. After he healed the man, it was Jesus who said, "Listen, don't tell anyone about this. But go straight to the priest and let him examine you; then in order to prove to everyone that you are cured, offer the sacrifice that Moses ordered" (Mark 1:44). The fact that this story is remembered in Matthew and Luke may help reinforce this posture on the part of Jesus.

To me this is not only "good news," it is great news! In these ways Jesus, who is referred to by the writer of Hebrews as the "author and finisher of our faith," demonstrates how we also are to be led by the Holy Spirit. We too are gifted with the same presence of God within us, so we can grow from the traditions and experience of our ancestors to acquire the power of God in our lives for today! Through our knowledge and through reverent study of the traditions of our fore-bears as demonstrated by Jesus, the Holy Spirit will bring to our understanding new and appropriate traditions for our time. We can only grow in God's grace as long as we also study and treasure the traditions, but strongly resist the pressures of traditionalism! Jesus makes it clear that it is not heresy to reject traditionalism, but that it could be very deadly to resist the Holy Spirit. Perhaps as we look at the life of Jesus we will see even more clearly how God's Spirit and traditions become an excellent source for realizing the abundant life. We also might see how deadly it is to accede to traditionalism!

Change is absolutely necessary if we are to grow and advance. For many people, however, change is difficult. Many Christian communities are very resistant to change. Someone has said that the seven last words of the church are "we never did it that way before!" This is another vivid example of the difference between tradition and traditionalism. The "tradition" for living is to learn how to accept the necessary changes one must experience in life. "Traditionalism" prevents individuals and groups from making these changes and becomes the destructive force that prevents new life. A living person or community cannot stay the same. They may honor and respect traditions from the past, but they cannot experience them in the same way day after day. There is no aspect or facet of our lives exempt from change. We must change in thought, word, and deed.

Chapter 2
Tradition in the Life of Jesus

Jesus was clearly a part of the Hebrew tradition. His parents are said to have kept appropriate traditions for him from the start. Like most Christian parents today who have their children baptized in the church, Jesus' parents followed their Jewish tradition of circumcision and presented Jesus in the temple soon after his birth. It is Luke who tells us, "A week later, when the time came for the baby to be circumcised, he was named Jesus, the name which the angel had given him before he had been conceived." Luke also tells us, immediately following in chapter two, that Joseph and Mary took Jesus to Jerusalem to present him to the Lord and perform the ceremony of purification as the Law of Moses commanded.

The ceremony of purification, according to Leviticus chapter twelve, is required for every woman who has recently given birth to a son or daughter, and it shows us that, from the beginning, Jesus' parents were an example of faithful, religious people who followed the traditions of their faith. They were not only faithful for themselves but for their child as well. While they were in the temple for Mary's purification, they also followed the prescription to dedicate their first-born son to God as was expected according to Jewish tradition recorded in Exodus chapter thirteen, "The Lord said to Moses, 'Dedicate all the first-born males to me, for every first-born male Israelite and every first-born male animal belongs to me." Their faithfulness in carrying out all the traditions relating to the birth of their son may also be an example of an important thought found in Proverbs, "Teach a child how they should live, and they will remember it all their life." While few in number, the earliest stories of young Jesus tell of his interest in tradition, especially the religious traditions of his people.

A story familiar to most people is Luke's story of Jesus' family traveling from Jerusalem after the Passover festival. On their return from the feast, they were unable to find him. When they went back to Jerusalem to search for him, Jesus was in the temple sitting with the Jewish teachers, listening to them and asking them questions. When his parents, who were very worried, found him, they impressed upon

Jesus their terror and wondered why Jesus would do such a thing. In answer, Luke has Jesus simply saying, "Didn't you know that I had to be in my Father's house?" They did not fully understand this answer, nor do we, but Luke tells us, "Jesus went back with them to Nazareth, where he was obedient to them."

When we met him as a man, however, we can see that his passion and respect for the customs and traditions of his people has only grown. In several places we are told that he was found daily in the temple. His early love for God's house was not lost as he became an adult. In fact, in some stories he is portrayed as a zealot for his love of this holy place.

Almost everyone remembers the story of Jesus going into the temple and driving out the merchants. In fact, this story is recorded in every one of the four Gospels. While there are differences, they are rather similar regarding the central point The major difference between them is that John places this event at the beginning of Jesus' ministry, while Matthew, Mark, and Luke place it at the end of Jesus' ministry, just before his triumphal entry into Jerusalem. They all have Jesus saying that the temple is to be a house of prayer (Mark alone adds, "a house of prayer for all people"), but that those who were desecrating the temple had turned it into a hideout for thieves! Were not these "desecraters" simply providing a necessary service? The people needed cattle, sheep, and pigeons in order to provide an acceptable offering in the temple. Those who came from a distance also needed to change their foreign currency into Galilean shekels or temple currency in order to pay the required temple tax. Hence some of the desecraters were named moneychangers along with those who were identified as vendors. These services, however, had become an established custom at the entrance of the temple, especially for the holy days. Why was Jesus so angry at this tradition? One attempt at an answer to this is in John's Gospel. This Gospel writer has Jesus' disciples remembering a portion of Psalm Sixty-nine, "My devotion to your house, 0 God, bums in me like a fire." Not really an answer as much as a claim to Jesus' zealous passion for the holy place of prayer and worship. Without the commentaries on this passage we might not have any answers at all. They are rich with explanations of the corruption which had developed over the years and which may have been peaking during this period. They list many circumstances, such as: unfair methods of tax collection, the rejection of cheaper animals for sacrifice purchased outside the temple with the insistence they be replaced with more expensive ones being sold within the confines of the temple, the noise and clutter that probably prevented many from actually praying or worshipping, especially the Gentiles, in whose court these exchanges were taking place.

Regardless of how we interpret this popular story, there is no doubt that Jesus was indeed passionate about his faith and that of his forebears. I believe, however, that this is a splendid example of the difference between tradition and traditionalism. I believe that it was to this end that Jesus was so passionately opposed! These customs, which surely were developed for the people's convenience to make the offerings necessary for holy sacrifice more easily available, as convenient as that may have become, had become a part of the traditionalism Jesus strongly rejected. Traditions, like many practices that start with a good purpose, grow into traditionalism and become corrupt, causing pain and sorrow to God and people. The traditions of worship and prayer too often become corrupt. Instead of bringing life and peace, they begin to bring death and oppression. Instead of focusing on God and the wisdom of God for direction, they focus on individuals and rules and regulations said to foster righteousness. Instead of pointing to the giver and the variety of gifts, we become more aware of the "gifted" and become overly concerned with how much we can "get"!

Any religious tradition that focuses on "What is in it for me?" or "What can I get out of it?" is not in the historic tradition of Jesus or the ancient people of God. The whole purpose of worship and prayer is to help us serve God and each other. The words and actions of Jesus tell the whole story. In fact, for we who are Christians, the words and actions of Jesus are the whole story—the Gospel! In the Gospels of Matthew, Mark, and Luke, Jesus is reported to have said something like this: "Whoever wants to be first must place himself last of all and be the servant of all." This is appropriate for all who would be Christlike, since they have also quoted Jesus as having said, "I have not come to be served, but to serve." This is not only the tradition of Jesus, but also the universal tradition of God. For me, the story of Jesus cleansing the temple is very clear. Most of our places of worship need the same cleansing. We no longer follow the life-giving traditions of

God. We promote the life-threatening traditionalism of people. Most of our churches are filled with rules and regulations. Some of them are written down. Others, just as real, exist only in the customs of a particular place. Most of those over which we fight or divide are not really worth the effort and are certainly not a part of the real Gospel. Most of us fight over buildings, authority, membership, validity, and a host of other traditionalisms. When was the last time you heard of churches fighting or splitting over things that Jesus said were most important? Things like: "I was hungry but you would not feed me, thirsty but you would not give me a drink; I was a stranger but you would not welcome me in your homes, naked but you would not clothe me; I was sick and in prison but you would not take care of me." A lot of churches have been started after a split over "correct doctrine," but few have been formed because a congregation wasn't caring enough! We may claim we are following the traditions of Jesus, but sadly, many are only following the traditionalism of religion constructed by humans. No, Jesus was not a heretic. He followed the real tradition of God, who sent him. His was only an apparent heresy. The religious leaders opposed to Jesus were sadly mistaken. They had been swallowed up by traditionalism, and it was killing them and their followers. Traditionalism is deadly, and Jesus demonstrated how passionately we must avoid it. A true follower of Jesus may seem like a heretic today, but don't be fooled. Avoid traditionalism!

Chapter 3
Traditions in Churches

I can think of hundreds of rules and regulations that were followed as absolutes when I was young. It was clearly taught that you could not be a true Christian if you did certain things: smoke, drink, dance, play cards, attend the movies, curse, or swear. It was also very clear that other things were absolutely required if you were to be considered a true Christian: attending church regularly, reading your Bible, praying every day, actively engaging in witnessing, tithing 10 percent of your income, and a lot more. Women were given further restrictions: no short hair, no short sleeves, no short dresses, no pants, no permanents, no make-up, and a lot more. On Sundays we remained dressed for church because we were in church most of the day. There was Sunday school at 9:30 A.M., Worship at 11:00 a.m., Young People's Fellowship at 6:30 EM., and Evening Praise at 7:30 p.m. On some Sundays we might also have an afternoon service at 3:00 em. By the way, it was wrong to read a newspaper on Sunday, but who had time?

Not only was the demeanor of a person an important concern, but also the decor of the place in which one worshipped. Obviously some churches were stricter than others, but all of them usually stressed simplicity. Most of the churches I attended as a boy did not have stained-glass windows, candles, robes for the minister or the choir, cushions on the pews, or other such amenities. Often churches with such excesses were spoken against in sermons as lacking in the true spirit of God's presence that was primarily internal and hardly external, except in one's personal actions as a Christian. Some of the churches I attended did not even have musical instruments. They sang hymns and spiritual songs in their worship services, but they were sung a cappella. Even though the Bible talked about the use of the lute, the harp, and the tambourine, to name a few, they rejected the appropriateness of their use today. The human voice was clearly made by God and was the only instrument that could be used to praise God. Instruments constructed by human hands were not acceptable. Since I loved to play the piano and organ, this was a little too much for me to bear.

As I grew older, it was interesting to see how more and more of these strict rules were eventually changed or forgotten. The people who remain in these churches are not always cognizant of these many changes, especially newcomers and young people. Often people look back to the "good old days" without truly remembering some of the hardships that were imposed.

As we traveled down south with the Word of Life Fellowship, we found that most Evangelical Christians smoked. They grew tobacco and it was not regarded as a bad habit. In the North, the sermon would speak eloquently about the evils of smoking, but when we visited the South these "truths" were conveniently absent from any of the sermons. I was raised in an Italian family, and my grandfather raised grapes and made wine. While we used grape juice for communion in our Gospel Church, we were only able to drink the real stuff at home. Actually, we were not supposed to do that either, but it was hard to take wine out of an Italian household. I remember many sermons which tried to explain that Jesus turned the water at the wedding feast at Cana into grape juice, not wine. We were not able to cite the words in Scripture, "take a little wine for the stomach's sake," only those which proclaimed "strong drink as a mocker." Dancing was always wrong unless one was "dancing in the Spirit" in church, as was the custom in many of the Pentecostal churches. Playing cards was only wrong if you used a "real" deck. We were all right if we used a deck called "Rook," even though it could be used to play and gamble in the same manner as "real" cards. It was something about the "characters" portrayed on these cards that brought evil into the world and into your life if you used them.

It was not uncommon to hear our pastor tell us that other churches were steeped in "man-made" rules. Because these rules were not clearly spelled out in Scripture, they were ridiculed as being superfluous. The rules we were supposed to keep were seen as being very scriptural, even though they were not always mentioned specifically in the Bible either.

One of the basic problems with tradition in the church is that each church believes its traditions are impeccable while others are not. The tension between churches is high because of this attitude. Each church believes very strongly in "right" and "wrong"; they are right and everyone else is wrong. This was the same problem Jesus had in his day with the Sadducees and the Pharisees. Then and now there are various sects of Jews, and they are still at odds with one another. Christians simply have a greater number of separate groups who are at odds with one another. I have heard (most often when I was a Baptist), that there are over three hundred groups of Baptists in the United States, and only a few of them see eye to eye on all matters.

Most of the so-called conversions are simply members of one Christian persuasion switching to another. For one reason or another they become disenchanted with where they are and move where they believe the grass is greener. Those who change to another group believe they have done so because of some ontological truth important enough to make such a change.

The words in Scripture which speak of One Lord, One Faith, and One Baptism become rather meaningless. The call of Jesus to be one as he and the father are one is a moot point. The focus of our Christian life is less a relationship with God and one another and more of a technical battle of right and wrong. Tradition is placed before people. This was the issue with the Jewish leaders of Jesus' day when he healed people on the Sabbath. They lost the sense that the Sabbath was created for people, not the other way around.

Our loving God is primarily interested in people and their human condition in the world we have been given. Our relationship to that world and to one another is the main reason for the impetus of the Law. God's purpose was never to restrict us, but to free us to love one another and to treat one another as God loves and treats us. If we act out of such love, Jesus tells us, the whole of the Law will be satisfied and fulfilled. When will we learn to come together in the name of God and stop separating ourselves into warring groups because of our prejudiced interpretations? Whenever it does happen, we may be sure that a portion of the Lord's Prayer will be fulfilled in our midst, "Thy kingdom come, thy will be done on earth as it is in heaven."

Chapter 4
The Biblical Tradition

One of the reasons we often acquire traditionalism from our traditions is because we tend to believe that traditions always were as they are, and so they should always be! Certain groups, to establish and enforce religious traditionalism in our time, use the Bible, a collection of holy writings, which is our best resource for earlier traditions. As we said earlier, traditionalism is defined as "adherence to tradition as authority, especially in matters of religion; a system of philosophy according to which all knowledge of religious truth is derived from divine revelation and received by traditional instruction." The Bible is used in this fashion by most of our Christian groups who foster and enforce traditionalism! Perhaps they do this because they equate the Bible too closely with one of God's attributes. We need to remember that the Bible was not always here, as God has been. While God had no beginning, the Bible clearly did! It might also help us to remember that it is only God who is the same yesterday, today, and forever.

The Bible has changed in many ways since its inception. Not only did it change while it was being formed, it is clearly different in its presentation in the variety of translations we now have. I remember the confusion and fighting over the new translations as they came into being. Some people attributed their origin to a "communistic plot" to overthrow the Christian faith, while others said the "modernists" had altered Christian teaching to serve their devious purposes. Many of these "purists" talked about the authenticity of the Bible in its original languages, until most people became aware that we had no original copies. Sadly, for those who were in panic, the manuscripts we did have were not always the same, and there were varied opinions about which might be more authentic among them.

While it was funny in a way, it was no laughing matter. Some people, unfortunately, lost their faith and confidence in this wonderful collection of traditions because they were always trying to use these sacred words to establish traditionalism! Knowing something about the way the Bible began may be more important than you realize. The Bible not only had a beginning, it started as oral tradition. Before writing was invented, storytellers were sharing with their clans various versions of the stories we now read in the beginning of our Bibles. We have only remnants of some of this early variety, because fragments of these stories were collected and inscribed.

As you begin to study the early beginnings of Holy Scripture you can see this unfold before your eyes. Examples of this variety start in the first few chapters of Genesis. In this book of beginnings there are clearly two stories of creation. The first story of creation begins with Gen. 1:1 and ends with Gen. 2:3. It begins with, "In the beginning" and continues with a description of evening passing and morning coming to describe a progression of days or events. After God creates man and woman in this story, they are spoken of as equals and are said to have been made, male and female, "in God's image, after our likeness." They are both blessed and empowered to "replenish the earth, and subdue it" and to share dominion over every other living thing. Finally, we are told that God liked what was done and rested on the final or seventh day, making it and everything holy.

The second story of creation begins with Gen. 2:4 and ends with Gen. 2:25. There are several ways in which we can easily see these are two different stories. First, this story is dramatically different in the way man and woman are created. Here man is created from the dust of the ground, not in the "image" of God. This story goes into detail about God placing this person in the garden and has him naming and identifying almost everything before a woman comes into the picture. After God discovers his loneliness, Adam is put to sleep while God removes one of his ribs, from which a woman is made. She is clearly declared his helper and is called woman because she was taken out of the man. There is no hint of equality here, nor has she shared in any of the naming. As the story ends we are told that this is the reason a man leaves his father and mother and is united with his wife, and they become one. Perhaps the man left his family in earlier times, but as these stories moved toward history in the patriarchal system, it was the women who left her family to join her husband's family. This period started with Abraham, and **Webster's New World Dictionary** describes a patriarch as "the father and ruler of a family or tribe, as one of the founders of the ancient Hebrew families: in the Bible, Abraham, Isaac, Jacob, and Jacob's twelve sons were patriarchs."

The next most important aspect of the biblical tradition is knowing when and how it began to be written down. A written account of tradition is distinctly different from oral tradition. Keep in mind that books, as we now know them, were not in existence before the invention of the printing press. The Grolier electronic encyclopedia says that Johannes Gutenberg was the first person to invent the printing press. *The Gutenberg Bible,* occasionally called *The Mazarian Bible* (1450-55), was the first book to be printed in Europe. Before this time, books were not bound or printed in the manner to which we are accustomed.

The encyclopedia goes on to tell us about the evolution of writing systems. Evidently, some forms of what may be called writing go back thirty thousand years, but the evolution of full writing systems has taken place only during the past five thousand years. Earlier forms were usually pictograms or ideograms. There was no alphabet, nor any specific signs given to particular objects. So far scholars have discovered seven ancient civilizations in which the transference from picture writing to word writing took place: Sumaiia (3100 B.C.E.), Egyptian (3000 B.C.E.), Proto-Elamite (3000 B.C.E.), Proto-Indie (2200 B.C.E.), Cretan (2000 B.C.E.), Hittie (1500 B.C.E.), and Chinese (1500 B.C.E.).

The history of writing is a fascinating story that includes details regarding limited and full writing. Limited writing refers directly to the object or idea portrayed. Pictograms or ideograms call to mind an image or concept. Because of its simplicity, the reader does not need to know the language of the writer but can usually translate the signs directly into his or her own language. Full writing systems may be defined as those collections of arbitrary signs that can represent all the words of the language to which they are applied. To understand this system, the reader must be fully acquainted with the language. It is also helpful, and sometimes vital, that the reader be familiar with the life and time of the content.

It is essential for us to know that our Bible comes to us from almost all sources involved in the evolution of writing. While our Bibles today are clearly written in the mode of full writing, we need to remember that they didn't start out that way. Our Bible shares with us a wealth of our forebears' experiences with God and their world over many years and changes in culture, and it shares this with us in a tremendous variety of forms.

Even after many of the books in our Bibles were written down in full writing form, we still did not have a biblical tradition. Even after the biblical languages were fully developed, many years passed before the various books of our Bible were brought together in the full collection of our present biblical tradition. Many in the church took great care in choosing these books. Many people who love the Bible do not realize there were many books that were not chosen to be included in Holy Scripture as we now know it.

Before the various books of Holy Scripture were canonized, the authority came from the prophets and apostles themselves. In the early beginnings of the Christian Church, no one quoted from the New Testament for several reasons. First, the "authority" came from the people who were speaking. They were either the apostles themselves or people who knew them. They spoke with authority on the issues of the day to people who were aware of their connections and status. Secondly, early apologists for Christianity were talking to people who would not acknowledge the authority of any New Testament books even if they were cited. Many cultures and places did not consider the prophets and apostles who wrote our Scripture important enough to speak with any authority.

Eventually, by the fourth century, when time had distanced the existing tradition from the living authority of former years, people began to look to some kind of written code for authority. The various books and letters that made up the New Testament canon, which were recognized as having a close association with the apostles and those who were schooled by them, were in need of some kind of certification. Authority and canon- icity were two different issues in the early history of Christianity.

The early church at the councils of Hippo (393) and Carthage (397, 419) accepted as canonical a larger Old Testament than the Hebrew Canon. At the Reformation, Protestants accepted a shorter version with the books in slightly different order as those found in the Hebrew Bible. At the council of Trent (1546), Catholics also included works in the Old Testament that are often referred to as deutero-canonical books. The Orthodox, at the Synod of Jerusalem (1672), approved some of the Apocryphal books as well. So, as one can easily see, while there is a general consensus among Christians as to the authority of many of the books in our Bible, there is no perfect agreement on the Canon of Holy Scripture among all Christians.

Realizing that such a tradition is hard to establish, we should also remember that only a relatively few people would have been concerned with such matters. Until rather recently, most people were illiterate. Average people may not have known that these volumes existed, and even if they had, they certainly would not have been able to read them. Until the invention of printing and the production of *The Gutenberg Bible* in 1456, and other versions that followed, the books and traditions contained in Holy Scripture were actually known and experienced by relatively few.

The invention of printing and the increased availability of Bibles, along with the Reformation's emphasis on biblical rather than ecclesiastical authority, inevitably promoted vernacular translations of Holy Scripture. Old and long-established ways were beginning to pass away as new ideas and exciting developments helped develop what we now consider to be a strong biblical tradition among our Christian communities.

Another aspect of the growth of our biblical tradition is important as well. Before there was any clarity to our tradition of Holy Scripture, there were strong personalities and systems which held the people of God together. We all speak of the prophets and priests—the prophetic and the priestly liturgical traditions. The prophets were the individuals who spoke to the people on behalf of God, and the priests formed the community of intercessors between God and the people. They were the authority for a long time as the people moved from one generation to another.

There was another significant shift in tradition about the time of Jesus and the apostles. During the time of Jesus the rabbinical tradition was becoming more firmly established, but the priestly liturgical tradition was declining and would soon come to an end. Many of the people to whom Jesus spoke began to receive him as a rabbi. Jesus' role as a rabbi brought him both fame and infamy. In 70 b.c.e., not long after the historical time of Jesus, the temple was destroyed. It was during this time of the growing authority and popularity of rabbis that the biblical tradition had its real beginning in the life of God's people. Then, after the temple was destroyed, Holy Scripture moved into its new place of focus among the people of God.

Our Bible has had many more years of evolution from the time of Jesus until now. Perhaps even more changes have occurred in the life of Holy Scripture than we have noted before the Christian Era. So many, in fact, that they could become another volume or book. It is enough for me to point out here that there have been many traditions regarding Holy Scripture over many years. There was never a time when everyone among the people of God agreed with any of the traditions. It should be clear that we cannot take any tradition from any age and pretend that it always was or always will be the way we must accept the Bible. To do so is to become bound by traditionalism and no longer able to celebrate and appreciate the numerous traditions that make our Bible so special.

Chapter 5

The Anglican Tradition

I have been a part of the Anglican tradition for the last thirty-four years. I was not born into this tradition, but came to it as I grew in my faith and practice. From the former chapters you can sense that a lot was happening to me in body, mind, and spirit. While I came from a family that was not attached to the Episcopal Church, it was a family that encouraged me to think. I was the oldest son and the third generation of people who came from Italy and Europe. My ethnic background provided me with a rich heritage. I was encouraged to be active in every aspect of life and was expected to excel in whatever I became involved, and that is primarily what I did. As the oldest son I had a host of aunts and uncles who supported me and gave me strength and wisdom. It was our tradition to come together almost every Sunday at my paternal grandparents' home. We ate, talked, and played together in one fashion or another. In my early years, most of that family attended the same Gospel church every Sunday for at least three or four services.

I saw the Episcopal Church as one with a long and great history. As one matures, history becomes more important. Having strong roots that press back to antiquity tends to make one stronger in one's existential existence as one moves along life's path. I also saw in this church a strong urge to continually grow and develop. Change was not an evil to be feared, but a facility to keep one fresh and full of life. This church had a great lineage of thinking people. Part of the great heritage of this church was Oxford and Cambridge universities which continue to encourage their students in thoughtful growth and development. These schools recognize diversity and individual dignity, and people are given the tools for personal excellence. People are expected to excel with all of the supports that are necessary for such fulfillment. The Episcopal Church had a strong spiritual heritage that was not divorced from the symmetry of a common life.

I also saw and was impressed with the comprehensive inclusiveness of the Anglican Communion. No one person or special emphasis had brought this church into existence. Early Christian writings by Tertullian and Origen in the early days of the third century spoke about the established Christian presence in England. It is assumed that Christian communities were established even earlier than the third century. We also know that three English bishops were present at early councils of the Christian Church in Arles, Sardica, and Ariminum. While it is clear that St. Augustine came to England from Rome in 597 with other companions, he did not start a church but strengthened it and its relationship to the larger Church. Under his leadership the English Church moved from its Celtic and Gaelic customs to a broader Western Catholic heritage.

Most people are under the impression that the English Church is King Henry's church. They seem to have the impression that he started the Church of England under his rule when he could not get the pope to annul his marriage to Catherine of Aragon. The truth is that this was only one of the catalysts that made the English Parliament adopt rules between 1529 and 1536 making the Church in England a national Church independent of papal jurisdiction. Fbr approximately ninety years the Church struggled with its independence: the reattachment of the Church under Rome during the reign of Mary I, the reestablishment of the national Church under Elizabeth I, the attempt to end the monarchy under Oliver Cromwell with the execution of Charles I, and the restoration of England under Charles II. As I studied history it was clear to me that no one person established this Church. It was truly a Catholic and universal church that tried to adjust its corporate life to minister to its people and further the Gospel of God.

This does not mean that I believe the Episcopal Church to be a perfect church. I am not even trying to suggest that it is a better church than any other. It is, however, a church that has struggled over many years to know God and all the fullness that was to be given to us by our Creator. It is a church that is open to everyone who wishes to be included in a continuing quest for God's truth. It is a church that can accept and effect the essential changes that a lengthy life brings to the wholeness of one's experience. It is a church that is alive with God's power and spirit to energize growth in every facet of one's life. It is a church that can only point to God for its beginning and the presence of God to enable it to continue. It is akin to the love of God —for all time, in all places, for all people.

The government of this church is also amazing. It knows both the power of bishops and the power of a congregation. Again, it is truly an inclusive church *(both and),* not exclusive *(either or).* It recognizes and celebrates the presence of God from above and below. We are a hierarchical church and a congregational church. This is why we are often referred to as the "Bridge Church," because we are Catholic and Protestant at the same time. Because the people choose their bishops, their leadership is from the midst of those whom they serve. They are empowered to lead, because the office of a bishop is for life. This perpetuity is true for our priests and deacons as well. In the perpetuity of their ministries the people of God continually reflect on who they are and what they need to be as they gather in conventions. Locally, nationally, and universally, the people of God come together to deliberate and discuss, so they can appropriately select the best way to serve in their ever-changing world. Through worship, study, and prayer, the Episcopal Church remains alive with God's presence to make the necessary changes as we move forward toward each new decade and century. Hie history of our church is a living history. There may have been times when we were bogged down for a while, but soon we rose up to move forward again to serve God and one another.

By now you may begin to see how I appreciate the traditions of this church and rejoice in the fact that we have had little occasion to get stuck in traditionalism. Perhaps this is true because we tend to concentrate on God as our source rather than any other person, place, or possession. While this church is comprehensive and inclusive, no one person or period of time tends to dominate. We have always relied on Scripture, Tradition, and Reason as resources to guide us, but no one of them is raised to the level of the supreme. We tend to be people of faith and believe that God, through the use of these and other resources, will help us be in the right place for our time. In this sense we are probably truly charismatic. We are able to speak the words of God for this age even though they may seem to be strange expressions to those who are caught in a more distant time. Some may even think we are heretical in that we do not preface our truths with "The Bible says," or "The Church teaches," or "Common sense indicates." It is always our hope, however, to be aware of what the Bible says and what the Church teaches, and to consider rationally our patterns of word and deed before we walk too vigorously ahead.

To move ahead in this manner is too risky for many. This why traditionalism is so popular. It is always easier to say, "We have always done it this way," than to find a new and living way. These words have often been called the Seven Last Words of the Chinch. We are a people of habit. There is genuine comfort in what we are used to. It is easier for most people to "second a motion" than to make the motion. Many leaders are more comfortable in going along with the "will" of their people than proposing a new way. It is also easier to be reactive than proactive. Most people can find a thousand reasons why a suggestion should not be followed, but only a few are able to come up with a new and creative proposal. We worry that someone may "rock the boat," but fail to realize that no boat is motionless unless it is completely out of the water! Unfortunately, traditionalism has rendered many a congregation useless.

To learn from our tradition that God is alive and loving should encourage us to keep moving. Faith is not so much the accumulation of correct statements as it is the expression of a vital life. We are encouraged to put our faith into action. It is absolutely true that "Faith without works" is dead. Religious people in Jesus' day were often able to quote the right words, but they were short on expressing them appropriately in their daily living. The life of Christ is a living example of what the religious people of his day were not. He spoke with authority, because he demonstrated by his life what others only spoke about. Jesus was an irritation to all those people, especially the religious leaders of the day, who were caught in the mire of traditionalism. Our Lord is said to have proclaimed that he came to bring us abundant life. Any life that stays tire same, day after day, cannot be plentiful. This is why I have titled my book, *The Apparent Heresy of Jesus*. Obviously Jesus was not a heretic. The Church, in fact, claims that Jesus was without sin. He was not wrong to be alive and progressive. He could be no other way because he was full of the Spirit of the Living God. The Creator is in one way always the same, and yet brings about the continuing change and majesty of this universe. God is the one who makes us as we are and the one who urges us to move toward the ideal.

I was drawn to this church because I sensed it was a community of God that would enable and encourage me to become all that I was to be in the name of God. I did not believe it to be perfect, but it did not need to be. It was not better than any other church, it was one I believed would be best for me. I could sense the fresh air of its presence all around me, yet know I was walking on solid ground. For every aspect of my life I knew I would have good advice and counsel, but I also sensed the spirit of openness that would always be there to help me grow into what God was calling me to be. A church that was filled with history and tradition, but one that was never long to be stuck in the dilemma of traditionalism.

Chapter 6
What Is Normal?

What do we mean by "normal"? When we look in a dictionary, normal is defined as "conforming with or constituting an accepted standard, model, or pattern; especially corresponding to the median or average of a large group in type, appearance, achievement, function, development, etc.; natural; usual; standard, regular."

According to this definition, normal is what we define it to be and not what may exist in a natural way or natural form. Quite the opposite of what we "normally" think! Most people believe that what is normal is natural; the way nature intended it to be. But this is not the case. Normal is what we define someone or something to be. So what we mean by normal is not what we normally think it is. Normal is what society or tradition claims it to be.

With the progress of time traditions change, and what was considered normal in one time period is, perhaps, no longer thought to be normal in another time. There is a phrase in one of our hymns that I believe says it very well: "Time makes ancient truth uncouth." What was conceived as natural in one time may be considered quite unnatural in another. If we do not understand or accept this principle of change, we will find ourselves in a time warp. We may be trying to live in our present era with the standards of another time.

I believe this to be a problem for most religious people. As I have already explained, it is easy for religious people to be caught in the traditions of the past. This is what I have called traditionalism. From my observations, religious people tend to believe that nothing ever changes in the essential areas of their faith. As we have noted in former chapters, this is not true. Because changes in religious areas have tended to evolve very slowly, it is easy to forget that they have occurred at all. We dare not neglect these changes or try to pretend that they do not exist. When we try to keep old traditions in a new age, we experience the dilemma of traditionalism. If our concepts of normal and tradition do not change as we advance in time, we will have difficulty with the concepts of our present time. While change is difficult for many people, it is necessary for everyone if we are to be

29

true to our time. It is most important to recognize that nothing in our lives stays the same. Changes occur in every facet of our lives. To function appropriately as time moves on we must be aware of these changes, accept them, and live by them. The tradition of our time are just as important to us as the traditions of our ancestors were to them.

Perhaps an example of how we define a normal situation will help. In our school system we usually grade on a curve. This is how we define the normal or the average students as far as their grades are concerned. It is based on the bell curve. This system is modeled on a bell-shaped curve, a statistical curve resembling the outline of a flared bell, usually representing a normal frequency distribution, in this case, of student grades.

This model usually expresses the results in the familiar grades A through F. A, of course, is the best or highest and F is the lowest. The curve is drawn by statistically analyzing the grades of all who participated in a test. From the highest to the lowest, a curve is drawn to determine file average grade, usually represented by the letter C. according to the curve, each participant is assigned a grade. The majority at the apex of the bell curve will get a C. As the curve descends, some will receive a B on one side of the curve, while some on the other side will receive a D. Finally, a few will get an A and a few will get an F.

It is important to notice that the curve will change from test to test even among the same participants. Each time the curve will determine what we will, in that case, determine as "normal." The teacher then applies the new definition of normal as each test is graded. It is also important to notice that, while this method places most of the students in the normal range, it also forces the definition of the few who will receive high or failing grades. The curve automatically distributes the grades to be assigned from A through F.

It is not an uncommon experience for children, when they move from school to school, to find themselves on a different place on the curve. They will always be judged by their performance in comparison to their peers. As they move into a different group they will naturally compare differently. They could easily receive higher or lower grades depending on the standing of the curve that is drawn by their new group. If a child moves to an area where most other children are smarter, then that child's grades will be lower. If the new group is of lower expectation, then the child's grades could be considerably higher. So depending on where we live, we could be considered more or less intelligent. This is only one example of how the concept of ourselves can change from one place to another, even in our own time.

The bell curve is a familiar and customary way by which we define what is normal for our educational process in many schools. In the past, obviously, this was not the custom. For some schools, especially colleges, this custom is already passé. The way in which we determine these standards will probably never stay the same for very long. Those in the field of education are not only familiar with such changes, they must adapt to them if they are to continue to progress in their field.

The bell curve is a tradition used to determine what is normal or average. When the tradition of the bell curve passes out of use, then a new tradition will take its place and determine what will be considered normal or average. If one tries to maintain the bell curve standard beyond its time, then that person will become entrapped by traditionalism. The more stubborn such people become in trying to maintain old standards, the more uncomfortable they become. If they continue their stance, they not only bring discomfort to themselves, they also cause pain to others. If the tradition they are trying to maintain has been out of vogue long enough they will begin to bring destruction on themselves and others.

While the concept of the norm in education is changing, there are many other aspects of our lives that are experiencing the same drama of progress. While some areas are more noticeable and perhaps more painful, we should realize that all areas of our lives change with time.

One of the most anxious and visible aspects of our religious faith today is the rapidity with which change is occurring. The amount of knowledge and discovery in our world at one time was more static. It changed, but with such slowness that hardly anyone in any one generation was able to perceive it. As time went on, however, the speed of change became more rapid. As new changes have been developed and discovered, there has been a correlation of the speed of such changes as well. Probably more has changed in our world in the last ten years than in the last several hundred years.

Rapid changes in technology and communications over the last several decades have literally changed the culture of our world and its people. Hardly a society anywhere has not been dramatically affected. Local cultures are now being changed by more powerful global ideas and economic structures. Today, many nations are multicultural societies composed of numerous smaller subcultures. Almost all of our cultures today cross national boundaries.

Because religion is usually conservative by nature, it is probably feeling the effects of such rapid change more than other areas of our lives. Conservatives are traditionally those who are averse to rapid change and are more accustomed to striving for balance and order while avoiding extremes. Religious people are more comfortable promoting faith over reason, tradition over free inquiry, hierarchy over equality, collective values over individualism, and divine or natural law over secular law. Traditionalism, which is a part of most religions, sets forth strong statements of faith even though they may not be very rational. It encourages the practice of past traditions rather than openness to new forms or values. Traditionalism relies on the strength of authority, whether it is in human or written form, over a moving of God's spirit in all people of faith for the guidance of the community. It too often insists on divine law or natural law even when there is clear evidence in Holy Scripture that these laws were changed in later writings.

Religious people are famous for reminding us that God never changes, but they seem to forget that almost everything God made has changed. It is certainly true that God's love for me never changes, but it is also a fact that I have changed many times in my body, mind, and spirit over these many years of my life. It is also true that everything else in my world has changed over the years as well. The world of Abraham and Sara hardly compares to the world in which we live today. They could have never imagined what our world would be like today, even as we find it very difficult to actually capture what their world was like then.

With all of the information that is available to many of us today, it is hard for us to know what our world is like now and to begin to imagine what our world will be like tomorrow. In the days of our forebears, information was at a premium. Only the few who could read and write and who had the luxury of being schooled could even take the time to consider such matters. Today most of our people can read and write, and more and more are experiencing the massive amount of information that is freely available on the Web. Almost every culture alive today can share its information, wisdom, experience, and thoughts with everyone else on the globe we call Earth. At one time we may have legitimately asked, "Who is our neighbor?" Now we are beginning to recognize that everyone is our neighbor! Our connection to one another is literally only milliseconds away.

Because of these massive changes, traditionalism has become more repugnant to the average person. One of the many statements of frustration today might be, "Lead, follow, or get out of the way." Tradition cannot lead us. Tradition can only provide depth and knowledge to those who would become our leaders. Tradition gives us the sense as to how others followed new paths in their time, so we can move with the same firmness to face the future in ours. Traditionalism, however, only gets in the way and holds us to a day that will never dawn again.

What is normal? If I were to try to list what was normal to people in each successive year in the past, it would be the longest book in the world. So much has changed that no one could list it all. On the contrary, if I were to try to list what has never changed since the beginning of history, it might be the shortest book in the world. The simple point is that *normal* is what we make it, because it never remains the same.

In short, life is only normal when change is occurring. The tradition of any time or place can be a wonderful asset in helping us move forward in our time and place. The wisdom of the past can provide us with a rich resource for our movement toward the future. It is obviously not normal to lock ourselves into the past and attempt to make it our present. That is traditionalism, and it can be very destructive to our present and future. Religious people need to be reminded of this, just as Jesus warned the people of it in his day.

Chapter 7
Obtaining Godly Normality

Today we like to celebrate the basic oneness of almost every religion. We have a sense that it is common for the majority of religious communities to believe in and stress the love of God for all people. In spite of the continuing arguments we have with one another about many details of our religious expression in worship and ethics, we share a strong sense that we aU believe that God is love and that God wants us to love one another.

In our Christian expression of this truth we often point to Jesus when he reminded the religious leaders of his day regarding the "summary of the Law." He tells them clearly that the Law and teachings of the prophets are contained in the prerequisite to love God with all our hearts, minds, and souls, and to love our neighbors as we love ourselves. We also point to something we call "The Golden Rule," which admonishes us to treat others as we would have them treat us. This pervasive doctrine about God and the people of God has become a banner of understanding for almost all faiths. The words that carry the idea may vary, but the sentiment is the same. This, I believe, is a basic tradition in most religions.

Making this common understanding of religious traditions take expression in our lives is not, however, as simple as it is to say the words. There are, I believe, two basic reasons for this. We have probably all thought about one of these reasons, because our various faiths help us deal with it, yet the other segment, which is an equal part of this common understanding, may seldom come to mind.

The first difficulty is our own personal determination. To be fit in every aspect of our humanity, we must practice to do well in areas where we wish to be accomplished. It is important to remember that to maintain excellence in anything, we can never stop practicing. This basic principle of life is absolutely vital to our success in everything we consider important. No one can name any worthy area of life that does not require practice in order to maintain excellence. The most gifted people in sports, music, education, research, and whatever else you might name will all tell you that practice is absolutely essential to their success. Practice is also a great asset to those who may not be so naturally gifted. Practice and hard work can sometimes enable persons to do what no one ever expected they could.

Should there be any surprise, then, that one might need to practice one's faith? Many people, when you discover what they believe as a matter of faith, are not very careful as to how they actually live out their belief in their personal life. They use a multitude of excuses for their neglect. They appear to truly believe that faith is the one area of life that is automatically whole without practice or special attention. It should be further noted that when we neglect any area of our humanity, it is certain to diminish and decay. I am sure you are familiar with the popular saying, "Use it or lose it."

In our world today there is hardly an athlete participating in any sport who does not realize the need for exercise and practice. There are only a few months out of the year when vigorous team members are not busy doing something to actively, consciously, and consistently develop their abilities to remain members of the team. Attention is paid to their whole person in their capacity to function to the best of their ability. What they eat, how they think, and what they do as a team member is crucial. These beliefs and practices even exist in our young people who participate in Little League and many other similar games of sport. To be absent or neglectful in any way may mean expulsion from the team.

While this concept has always been popular in the world of athletics, it has become equally pervasive whenever excellence is to be obtained in almost any area of human existence. Those who excel in any discipline today will demonstrate the same commitment to persistence in developing their full potential as persons. Successful people today are happy to proclaim their commitment to their work, and even their play. There is a note of joy in their expression and accomplishment to reaping the rewards of winning. Many recognize that "All work and no play makes Johnny a dull boy," so successful people include all areas of their lives in their active pursuit of growth.

What about our active and purposeful practice in matters of faith? While many people are beginning to focus on such a need in their lives, the majority may be absenting themselves from it. When you consider the number of people who do not attend worship on any regular basis, you might begin to see what I mean. The God who

35

loves all and wants us all to love one another has encouraged us to gather together regularly. I am not aware of any religion that does not encourage its members to gather together on a regular basis, especially for prayer and worship. God has certainly been consistent on getting this message out clearly to every faith. Why then, when it comes to people's faith, do they insist they do not need this? Why are so many convinced they do not need anyone else in order to maintain a proper relationship with God?

People need to remember that God has called us to community. God wants us to live and work together. It is impossible to practice love and to establish an appropriate relationship to our world and the people in it when we remain isolated from one another. How many athletes would try to convince their coaches that they can practice and prepare for the game at home? How many team members would even enjoy this model? So much of the fun and joy is in the gathering of the team to prepare for the game.

Perhaps more people will begin to see that our world would be much improved if we could realize this truth in matters of faith. The people of God were not meant to be lonely. We need to be together in regular times of gathering if we are to be truly fit to serve God as qualified citizens. Isolation is a real danger to our health and well-being in every aspect of our common life. This is why traditionalism is a killer as well.

The traditions of our faith can be life-giving. Tradition, in the best sense, reminds us to come together and to love and support one another. It provides customs that enable us to acknowledge this in both our public and private lives. These structures of tradition help us set goals and encourage us to accomplish them. Traditionalism, as we have seen in former chapters, is the over-emphasis of any one tradition that is no longer capable of serving us in the present. Traditionalism keeps us from making progress and prevents us from moving into the future with a new grace and competence in the name of God. Traditionalism has a tendency to move us toward the worship of tradition, rather than to worship a living God who continually moves us toward maturity.

The second difficulty is that we forget our history and how it has made some dramatic changes in nearly every area of our lives. The traditions of the past are simply no longer the traditions of today. It is very important that we realize that change is normal. It is important to remember that, while God may never change, the world God has given to us never stops changing. We often lose sight of this fact, and when we do, we bring frustration at best, and devastation at worst to our lives. Unfortunately, many of our religious communities either refuse to acknowledge that change is normal or they are remiss in reminding us about such continuing changes in the totality of our lives.

Change is so pervasive and normal that it might be easier to think about what, if anything, has not changed. As I think about my world and my life, I cannot think of anything that has remained the same. Perhaps I would venture to say that God has not changed, but I would quickly have to add that our concept of God has dramatically changed over the years. When I was younger, many people were afraid of God. It was common to assume that the bad things that happened to us were a direct result of God's punishment for our behavior.

Our early ancestors were even willing to offer human sacrifices to appease the anger of their gods. The natural functions of nature would often scare people to death. They assumed that lightning, thunder, flood, drought, famine, diseases, death, and many other regular natural occurrences were a direct action on the part of a god who was angry. Less frequent but fairly regular natural cycles like the eclipse of the sun or moon, the appearance of a comet, or an earthquake or volcanic eruption would drive them to panic. Their lack of understanding of the world in which they lived caused them to invent traditions and ceremonies that might counteract these events and cause them to lessen or cease altogether.

Because changes in their knowledge and understanding of the world were slow at first, the traditions that were established for many of these happenings were in vogue for a long time. Until recently, change was rather slow. For years, most people were not able to read or write.

They did not attend school as we know it, nor did the majority have anything close to a formal education. Only a few were able to participate in research and development, while most labored hard just to stay alive. Only a few areas of larger population were privileged to have communities of people who were free to study and learn. While change was present, it was not apparent to most people. It was easy to believe in absolutes and to have the sense that tradition never changed. Traditionalism, as such, became the norm for many.

For a significant period of time, new ideas were actually condemned by those in authority. One of the most famous examples of this is Galileo. He developed a new understanding and vision of the world when he invented the telescope. He learned that the earth was not the center of things at all. He discovered the sun and other planets, and he began to speak about what he was learning. It was not too long before the leaders of his world began to silence him for trying to change the traditional understanding of his day. The traditionalism of his time was so profound that Galileo was condemned and excommunicated from the Church, which had tremendous authority and control. Until very recently he remained officially apart from the established authority as one who espoused evil and wrong. The fact that the Church only very recently reversed his status of separation demonstrates the reality of traditionalism and its persistence among us.

Traditionalism sets what was normal for a previous time as the standard for all time. Traditionalism is difficult to change at any time and therefore becomes a systemic problem, especially in religion. When an acceptable tradition is held for too long it often becomes the evil it was meant to expose. This fact is only made worse when change is more rapid.

When change occurred more slowly, over several generations, the effect of any tradition becoming fixed in time was also a slow process. Its effect would take years to become a serious problem for having been in existence for too long. Now that change takes place so rapidly, a tradition's usefulness or lack thereof becomes more notable and severe. In the last one hundred years the rapidity of change has increased dramatically. We now live in a world where changes take place before our eyes almost every day.

Most of the advances in technology, science, space, sociology, medicine, economics, and every other area of our lives you can name have happened in the last fifty years. With the invention of the computer and communications, we now see change happening every day. The speed of change is so rapid today that we have to actually work harder than ever before. There were predictions that we would all be working less and have more money by now, but the reverse is true. We can hardly keep up with what is happening daily in our lives. The amount of information presently available on the internet alone is beyond the comprehension of most people. There is probably no one alive who can absorb or utilize it all. In the light of these facts it is easy to see why tradition can hardly be around for very long.

From my point of view traditionalism is virtually impossible today. Even so, we are so used to having it in some aspect of our lives that we still think it can exist. Many people want to hang on to it so badly that they call those who become comfortable without it heretics. Many people have yet to become sufficiently cognizant of the rapidity of change, so they fail to recognize the transition from one tradition to another. Tradition just does not hang around for very long anymore. Changes occur so rapidly today that they may abolish traditionalism and cause panic similar to that experienced by our ancestors. They lacked understanding because few were given the privilege to partici- pate in the opportunity to understand, but our weakness may be our inability to change our understanding often enough to keep up with the immense growth of knowledge that exists today.

To obtain a Godly normality today we need to recognize and cel- ebrate that traditionalism is dead and that traditions are a passing fancy. We best learn to hang on to God and to one another so we can move ahead with relationships that count. Our love for God and for one another is how Jesus said his true disciples would be known in God's realm.

Chapter 8
Our Personal Tradition

Most of life is a matter of perspective. We each learn to look at things from different points of view even when we think we are a part of a special community or cultural experience. Each of us moves at our own pace. It is like the story of an accident between the turtle and the snail. The police were called to the scene, and one of the officers asked the snail, "What happened?" The snail thought for a moment, then answered, "I don't know really, it all happened so suddenly!"

Most of us tend to feel that life moves rather quickly. So often we hear others exclaim how quickly a season or year has passed. How time flies, we exclaim when we are involved, and especially when we are enjoying our life experience. Our experience of life seems to move along faster than we can believe. No matter what our perception, life is sure to move on. Along the continuum of life's progress we become who we are. Our ideas and customs take on new shapes from day to day. We may not always be cognizant of the process, but the process takes place nonetheless.

Because we are not always consciously aware of this process and because it seems to pass by so quickly for most of us, it should not surprise us that we are not always aware of how we have arrived at our present place. Many people are simply unaware of their traditions and how they have come to adopt them. We assume that we are simply who we are. Unless our habits or thought patterns are challenged, or unless we are moved to write a biography of our lives, we may never give any thought at all to how we became the way we are. When our thoughts and patterns of living are seldom challenged or questioned by others or ourselves, it is only natural that we function as traditionalists. It is not hard to become firm in our ways and to get really annoyed when we are questioned, if we are not used to such challenges.

The majority of people do not find it pleasurable to be challenged with regard to their thoughts or habits, so we tend to live in communities and have friends who are like-minded. We like to be comfortable and live as easily as possible. It is only natural that we choose to be with people who are most like us. If we can, we choose our churches, our clubs and associations, our entertainment, and our work environment to be places that bring us comfort, not challenge. It is not uncommon for people to drift away from or eliminate entirely situations or circumstances that bring them annoyance. This might be the primary reason why so many drop out of school or quit their jobs. It may be difficult to acknowledge how resistant most of us are to such discomfort and challenge.

As I have shared with you in previous chapters, there were many circumstances and opportunities that enabled me to be alert and pay attention to many aspects of my life in thought, word, and deed. By now you should know that I am "over the hill" (over fifty years old), so my life has been full and there have been many changes. Because some of my life experiences were not common or complacent, I have been able to observe these happenings with deep thought and notice. In many cases I was forced to change. Life would not allow me to simply pass through in a casual way. In almost every year of my life I have encountered significant circumstances which caused dramatic change. I am grateful that most of these times caused very positive and productive changes, so I must be extremely thankful to what I firmly believe was the leadership of God in my life. Change, in many ways, has become a natural way of existence for me.

I considered writing about many of these happenings in this book, but then I realized how long this book might become. I also realized it would be complicated, so I decided I would rather have you read what I am trying to say by keeping it short. If this book became too complicated it could detract from the fact that my faith is comprehensive yet simple. I rejoice in God's marvelous gift to the world through Jesus Christ, and I desire that you also may rejoice in this Good News. I hope my personal tradition will assist you in reaching your simple and profound connection to this wonderful message of grace and love. I hope it will help you claim and acknowledge your own personal tradition as you have known and received it. I now enjoy the freedom of a living personal tradition, and I celebrate the loss of any traditionalism.

My life has now become rather sacramental. We say that a Sacrament is an outward and visible sign of an inward and invisible grace. What I tend to do now in an outward and visible way is the product of an inward and personal relationship with the One who was,

41

and is, and always will be. This personal relationship is no longer complicated, nor is it based on anything but a living relationship with God. It is, as the Scripture says, a gift from God, not anything we have done or could do. It is, of course, not without principle or substance, but constantly aware that neither principles nor substance can ever bring life. As this life in me grows, everything continues to be changed and renewed. This living, loving relationship with God is what brings new life, now and forever.

May I suggest that there are two primary concepts that form the true and unique core of the Christian Gospel: love and eternal life! To me, these are the primary gifts that Christianity brings to the world. There are many other words of wisdom and knowledge God has given to humankind, and they are shared with us in other traditions so we can appreciate and understand them. When we believe that our Christian tradition is the only bearer of God's wisdom, we are guilty of the pride that God told us could cause us to stumble or fall. Since the beginning of human life, God has faithfully spoken to people and has consistently shared wisdom and knowledge. This book needs only to remind us of our share and contribution to this stream of revelation. When the time was right, the Scripture says, God sent the Living Word to us to complete and begin this personal experience of abundant and eternal life.

To delineate the fullness of what I mean, let me share some thoughts and experiences that may help clarify my position. There is an emphasis in our faith that, I believe, holds us back from the beauty and actuality of God's love for us. What I am about to say may shock you at first, but please hear me out as I try to portray and complete what it is I wish to say. I want to bring your attention to another way in which a meaningful tradition of our past has become embedded in what I would call traditionalism. Let me share some thoughts and experiences about the cross.

The cross has become the basic symbol of the Christian faith. One can hardly go to a Christian church without seeing or hearing about the cross. I am not sure if we realize how much we have focused on this aspect of our faith. To many, both Christian and non-Christian, the cross represents the sum and substance of the Christian faith. There is a lot more I wish to say about this tradition, but let me stop for a moment and ask if you believe that the cross of Christ should be the main symbol of our faith. If my guess is right, you may be wondering how any Christian could even ask such a question. Why would anyone who claims to be a Christian ever question the centrality of the cross?

Well, let me ask another question. Can you think of anything else that might be more central to the Christian faith? I can. I personally believe that the Resurrection of Christ is much more central to our faith. The first and foremost holy day in the Christian Church is Easter, the day we celebrate the Resurrection. When we study the development of the Christian year, all of the other feast days historically came later and developed from Easter. It was so powerful in the life of the early Church that they changed their day of worship from the Sabbath to Sunday, the first day of the week. The apostolic writings even claim that if Christ was not raised from the dead, our faith would be worthless and empty. I hope these brief statements, which can be amplified at length, will give you witness as to why I see the Day of the Resurrection as the primary focus for all Christians.

Am I trying to suggest that we do away with the sign of the cross? Of course not! I am suggesting, however, that we have become involved in traditionalism when it comes to the cross. I have been saying all along that tradition, when it becomes traditionalism, can be a detriment at worst and a hindrance at best. I believe that many Christians today have been caught up in traditionalism when it comes to the cross and its current uses in thought, word, and deed. Let me share some additional reasons why I believe this.

The various ways Christians use the symbol of the cross has actually become a source of division among us as Christians. In earlier chapters, especially in chapters one and three, I shared various differences and approaches in my experience of Christian teaching as I grew up and moved from one Christian tradition to another. In my earlier years it was common for me to hear that other Christians did not have the true or full understanding of the Gospel. They held strong and different views of the cross. Some Christian communities would not even have the symbol of the cross visible in their worship space; either because they claimed to worship a living Christ or because they did not believe in the use of symbols. Others had a cross visible, but it was plain and empty. Others told me that Roman Catholics worshipped a dead Christ because they usually had a crucifix as their symbol. Some even suggested that Roman Catholics might not believe in the Resurrection.

I remember that when I was coming into the Episcopal Church I began to wear a symbol of Christ the King about my neck. Even though this form of the cross represented the power of a risen and ascended Lord, one of my aunts found it inappropriate. At first she saw it as a sort of rabbit's foot; something that was worn to save me from accidents and the like. When I assured her it was not like that, she wished it were at least an empty cross, without the figure of Christ. Then we talked about the many Christians we knew who had bumper stickers saying, "Christ died for our sins," and how this seemed to be all right. I wondered why it was acceptable when it was in written form, and why it became wrong and offensive when it appeared in three-dimensional art. It helped a little, but she still could not understand why I had to wear it at all to express my progressive life in Christ as an Episcopalian. Then we talked about wedding rings and why people needed or wanted to wear them as symbols of their marriage. It was not necessary, nor was it wrong; it was simply a tradition.

As time went on, I also noticed something else. While fundamentalist or evangelical Christians, as they were called, tended to think that Roman Catholics focused on the death of Christ because of their pervasive use of the crucifix, they were not really looking at their own tradition in words and music. It was sort of like the pot calling the kettle black. Take a good look at the hymn book and notice how many songs mention or focus on the cross and the theme of death and dying; the death of Christ, our need to die to self and take up our own cross of trouble and eventual death. There are, in comparison, very few hymns that speak of the Resurrection and challenge us to new life. I believe we need many more hymns that invite and call us to new life, change, growth, and development; rehearsing the promise that we are alive for evermore. We need to remember that words are symbols. They dramatize our hopes and our beliefs. Just because some Christians do not use other forms of art to depict the death of Christ does not preclude their consistent attachment to a similar theme.

I further began to recognize that the use of this theme increased the Church's ability to try to control the lives of its congregants. Continually remembering and emphasizing that Christ died for our sins enables the leaders to consistently remind us of our guilt. This technique also provides an excellent opportunity to call into question the way we live our lives. It allows what we commonly refer to as legalism, and it gives the church power to make rules for the way we must live. Need I remind you that almost every church has rules and regulations, and that one cannot be a good member unless one conforms? The more the members conform to the rules and judgments of their church, the higher their esteem among the people. The power of the Church becomes clear and corruption tends to abound. Martin Luther was just one of many to point out these abuses, and the continual need for people such as Luther even in our day goes without question. The role of the Christian community was never to have control over our lives, but to teach and motivate us to receive and utilize the power of God to live abundantly in all aspects of our life.

Our Lord came to bring life and wanted everyone to experience life in abundance. When we emphasize the wrong aspects of our faith we tend to lose sight of this goal. Certainly Jesus needed to die in order to be raised to life again, but his death was actually a small prerequisite to the main purpose of his coming. God sent Christ to be the living Word. He was not sent to condemn us but to enable us to have life, now and forever. Our values for life are seen in the way he lived among us. Our principles for life were noted in the words he spoke. Our example of the longevity of this life was demonstrated in the Resurrection. The values and principles that Jesus taught were not for this life only, but for all eternity. The sooner we accept this positive way of existence, the longer we will have to make progress in a life that is truly satisfying and life-giving.

I wish I had learned this a long time ago. It is so easy for people to be negative and to complain. This is true in our spiritual life as well. We need teaching and worship that reminds us to be positive and encourages us to "get over it" and rise above every circumstance. Unfortunately, much of what we do and say in our churches only helps us to remember and repent. Certainly there is nothing wrong with repentance, but repentance should never be the main course. It, like the death of Jesus, should only be a small but important fact along the way. The greater values of the Gospel are contained in stories and, most especially, the Resurrection of Christ. This is what it all leads up to. To get stuck at any point along the way is to get bogged down in tradition, which then becomes traditionalism, and traditionalism can never bring life.

I believe it is time for every Christian and for the entire Christian community to get back to the main point, the resurrection. Our songs, our teachings, our thoughts, and our actions all must more consistently reflect this major theme of life eternal. The power of Christ in us is not to control or to thwart us. We are prevented by many other circumstances and powers in the world, along with the weakness of our own humanity without God. The power of God is made available to us by gift and, when we receive this gift as it is uniquely brought to us in Jesus Christ, we are inspired and empowered to life abundant. It is like a famous secular song which speaks of our longing for a place where "seldom is heard a discouraging word and the skies are not cloudy all day." Why are so many of our churches caught up in traditionalism? Isn't it time our churches became an open field in which we might roam (whether with buffalo or not) and develop to our fullness in positive ways in the name of God?

To emphasize my point, our religious communities should be encouraging us to develop our personal traditions and enabling us toward maturity in godly ways. Like good parents, we need to be supported as we grow to become the people that God has called us to be, not simply to follow in our parent's footsteps as cloned human beings. Traditions show us the way and enable us to form new traditions for our time. Traditionalism defines the way everyone must be at all times and eliminates growth. Good community traditions, when they are not worshipped or preserved, foster the development of better traditions for a new day.

Chapter 9
The Danger of Traditionalism

One of the phrases often attributed to Jesus is that he came to bring life in abundance to everyone. This intention is certainly backed up when we consider the stories and circumstances surrounding his life. There were many occasions when others came to him to complain about his words and actions. Jesus did not always seem to abide by the established traditions of his day, especially the ones that were on the verge of becoming examples of traditionalism. Jesus would rise above these nay sayers by pointing to a higher authority or larger vision of life and well-being. To his critics' dismay, he would move forward to encourage and to heal, establishing the intention of God toward wholeness for all humankind.

In most cases, a tradition enables; traditionalism, far too often disables or may even bring death. While some who leaned toward traditionalism may have considered Jesus a heretic, he tried to declare his intention toward life. His emphasis was on the love of God and the power of that love to bring everyone into a living relationship with God and with others. Traditions may evolve from our interactions with friends and family, but traditions are hardly ever the cause or the glue that holds friendships together. When a friendship begins to depend on habits or traditions, you will notice a loss in the intensity and depth of that relationship. I would further assert that when habits or traditions turn into traditionalism, it is impossible for personal relationships to have depth, and the possibility for vitality and spontaneity is completely gone.

The magic of what God intends for us and what Jesus' ministry envisioned is based on love, an inward and invisible grace that brings forth outward and visible results. The Sacraments, when appropriately celebrated in community, become a small picture to enable us to grasp the depth and fullness of this living reality in our human existence. Worship sets the stage and opens the doors to the probability of our going forth from the gathered community to experience this lifestyle on a daily basis. Each of us, therefore, must determine how often we need this gathering to maintain our focus and encourage-

47

ment to continue to live daily in the abundance of God's grace. This is why worship is so necessary in our lives. It is extremely important that we gather on a regular basis with others to acknowledge that God is the source of our life. We cannot live well without coming together to feed from God's holy table on all the resources we need to grow and prosper. We need to be continually empowered and reminded to share our gifts and resources with our neighbors. To neglect this invitation and celebration only causes us to lack what God and others can bring to us.

While every community may develop forms or traditions that constitute a basic framework for their worship, these traditions must remain flexible. If any tradition becomes so important it becomes the focus, rattier than enabling those gathered to enter a life-giving experience with God and the others gathered, that tradition no longer brings life. When a leader—or anyone in the community—begins to maintain a tradition because it is a tradition, then it becomes traditionalism. When this primary position is given to any tradition it clearly becomes idolatry. The worship of the way one worships becomes greater than God, who alone should be primary. When this happens, no matter hi what church or denomination, we sense that the community is dead. This is why I said earlier that traditionalism far too often disables or even brings death.

The danger of death is not only to the community. An individual caught in the net of traditionalism may also face death. The experience of death can be incomplete or complete. An incomplete death is the more usual experience. This is when a person's mind or spirit is affected but they do not experience an actual physical death. If the pain created in the mind or spirit is sufficient, that person may actually take their life in an action we call suicide. Unfortunately there are too many of these happenings year after year. You may be aware of someone who was so devastated by his or her life circumstances.

Unfortunately, my mother was affected in this way. It took many years of emotional and physical illness, but it happened. I am including my observations regarding her sad demise because they illustrate my experience of how devastating traditionalism can be in a person's life. Her pain was a strong influence for change in my life. It was a hard lesson that took a long time to analyze and filter, but it was one of the most significant moments in my movement toward an abundant life for myself. I will be brief, but I hope to bring a sufficient summary of what I learned to make a very important point.

In my earlier years my mother seemed bright and cheerful. She was busy caring for my sister and me and, of course, for my father. Her talents were many and varied. Whatever she did she did well. She did nothing halfheartedly. Our home was always kept clean and neat. She not only prepared all our meals, but she made a lot of our clothes and the decorations for our home. She was able to make drapes, recover chairs, upholster, make rugs, and even paint and wallpaper. Her interests and activities extended beyond our home and family to our church and community. She loved people and enjoyed doing things with them and for them. Both my father and my mother were engaged actively in the wider community, and this brought us into contact with many people. This was in addition to our being an integral part of a large family on my father's side and a modest sized family on my mother's side. It was a wonderful and enriching experience for my sister and me. My mother and father were wonderful parents, and I am extremely grateful to have been born to them.

As I was growing older, especially during my years in high school, I began to realize that my mother had dreams of her own; dreams that present traditions would not allow and could not bless. There were several dreams, but the most vivid was to use her vocal abilities in a professional way. For years she took voice lessons, even while I was in grammar school. Her dream was to eventually sing in the opera. As I was growing up, I would accompany her on the piano or organ. She was popular as a soloist and was invited to sing in many churches and on religious occasions. She sang on radio and television and probably never said no to any opportunity she was given, but she knew when she had to say no.

Our traditions held her back and prevented her from becoming what she might have been. We were very religious, and our religious faith was very narrowing and confining. In addition, it was not a time when most mothers would be found working or actively involved in a professional career. In spite of my mother's aspirations, she was given no encouragement. In fact, there were strong male figures in our family who strongly discouraged her from following her dreams. Religious inhibitions and the cultural climate of our family were strong deterrents.

The third factor that, I believe, brought about her demise was an unfortunate physical problem with her back. After a long search for a solution, she underwent an operation for a fusion of the spine. At the time this was a rather risky operation, but there appeared to be no other solution for her extreme pain and deterioration. It was also determined, probably too late, that medications during and after her surgery were doing her more harm than good. This added burden began to wear on her spirit.

In the midst of this physical pain, her father added an additional level to her pain. My mother was his oldest child and, while I am sure he loved her very much, he always held her and her family to a higher standard. My grandfather was an Assemblies of God minister who was very conservative in his thoughts and ways. Like most religious people, however, his preaching did not always coincide with his lifestyle. While he fervently preached against television, he would watch it in our home each Monday when he visited us on his day off. While my mother was in the hospital recovering from her spinal operation, he explained to her that God might have healed her if she had been a stricter mother and more careful to exclude unwholesome activities such as television from our home.

Many traditions of that nature had become traditionalism in the minds and hearts of too many of our close relatives. As times changed, they could not change at all. Today when I mingle with members of similar churches, I am amazed at how open and progressive they have become. By today's standards they are still quite conservative, but they have learned to let go of many of the former traditionalisms of my day.

The sad day came in September of 1966, when I was called home to find that my mother had taken her life. She had threatened it many times, but we never thought it would happen. In addition to our grief, we had to struggle with the fact that many in our circle believed that those who took their own lives were surely doomed for eternity. Some churches would not even allow them to be buried with the blessings of the church. I had a lot to think about and I did a lot of thinking.

I am certainly not blaming my mother's death simply on the oppression imposed by traditionalism. There were obviously many factors involved, which is true when anyone commits suicide. Life is usually complicated, but one might expect one's religious community to be a source of hope and encouragement, not of oppression and condemnation.

During this time, I too was going through some inward turmoil. While I never thought of taking my own life, I knew some people in similar circumstances who had tried to take their lives. I was struggling with the fact that I was a homosexual. This was, to say the least, not a happy thought or feeling for one who was born in an Italian Pentecostal family, and it caused me a lot of personal tension and anguish. While times have changed and there is now some acceptance for us today, this was almost forty years ago, and the climate for any tolerance was dangerously poor. I cannot even begin to find the words to express how alone and devastated I was at the time. I literally had no one to talk to about this problem.

I am still amazed that anyone would begin to believe that someone would ever "choose," as they say, this life-style. I can assure you that it is not a choice; it is simply a fact of life. Without going into detail, I can tell you that I did everything one could at the time to try to be a heterosexual. Even though, at the time, homosexuality was on a list of sicknesses compiled by the medical world, I knew I had more than a sickness. As I eventually have come to understand, I did not choose to be gay. I did not wake up one morning and decide to be gay any more than heterosexual people wake up one morning and decide to be straight. I did not then, nor have I ever, traveled with people or to places where I had any contact with homosexuals. There was no chance that 1 was coerced or converted to a life-style. I grew up in a very strict religious world and was very active in the church all my life. My homosexuality was something that was a part of me from an early age; something I now had to learn to live with and accept.

I do not wish to get off the subject by spending a lot of time talking about my growing up and coming to terms with whom I am. Many good books and intelligent studies can do this much better than I can. I wish I had the words to tell you how God spoke to me through many people and on many occasions to let me know how much I was loved, just the way God made me. The main point I wish to make here is that my religious experience was not a life-giving experience; it was more like a death sentence. The traditionalism that is still prevalent today among many churches could have led to my demise. In plain English, it was a killer!

I remember that those who held strong views about anything they believed to be opposed to Scripture would often quote a verse from Hebrews, which said that the word of God was quick and powerful, and sharper than any two-edged sword. They seemed to delight in using Scripture as if it were a sword to cut people like me to pieces. They seemed to be more interested in maintaining purity of doctrine than the well-being of people. They seemed to be unfamiliar with the fact that Scripture's reference to the Word of God was to Jesus Christ, not to the written words. In spite of the many stories in which Jesus was kind to people whom religious leaders would consider enemies, they preferred to believe that Jesus would have cast out the evil that, from their point of view, possessed people like me.

Psychiatry notes that people who try to take their lives are, more often than not, crying out in a desperate way for help, but people in religious traditionalism simply discount this as a worldly theory. Homosexuality has been removed from Psychiatric Association lists of illnesses, but people in religious traditionalism simply discount this as a theory against the will of God. Even though there is no record in the Gospels that Jesus ever said anything about this (though the writings of Paul written soon after Jesus' death speaks about it), they grab a verse from wherever they can to make it the most terrible of sexual sins. Even though the context surrounding verses they do cite have changed in meaning and interpretation over the years, religious traditionalist maintain the correctness of a former tradition.

It is not uncommon for traditionalists to use a popular phrase in Scripture that claims people can be known or judged by their fruits. I have been in the ordained ministry for over thirty-five years, and I would like them to look at the fruits of my ministry. Even though I can testify that God has blessed me over and over again in my ministry, and even though the evidence may back up what I say, they will tend to do their best to diminish or absolutely denigrate what they hear and see. These people continue to use their sharp swords to choose and lift from the Scriptures, and in doing so, they kill and wipe out what God has made and used from generation to generation. Some people today believe we should re-establish the temple in Jerusalem and again offer animal sacrifices as the proper worship of God, even though many stories and words in Scripture tell us God does not desire this. Religious traditionalists cannot be persuaded, even though so many more of God's people have seen the light. They claim, as some did in the near past, to be the "moral majority" when they are not necessarily more moral than others, and they were certainly never a majority.

Chapter 10
A Living Tradition

When we are told in the Gospels that Jesus said he had come to bring us life in all its fullness, we have a hint of the divine intention and gift that came through Jesus. Because the primary holy day in Christianity is Easter, we have a demonstration of the scope and quality of this life. The life that God intends and extends to us is neither temporary nor anemic. It is an on-going process filled with enormous possibilities which are universal in scope with eternal dimensions. God's gift of abundant life is beyond all comprehension when you remember the promise that the same Spirit who raised Jesus from death will also give life to our mortality. The fact that God never leaves us or forsakes us in this life or the life to come is overwhelming to people who have not yet grasped the scope of God's love and caring for all people.

Before we go further, let me admit that life can be frustrating and strenuous. There are days when we feel as though we are being put to death. I am not claiming that I have never had those human and debilitating feelings. This mortal life is tough from beginning to end; that is why it is often referred to as the school of hard knocks. At this point, I would only ask you to recall the Gospel stories of Jesus' life. Did he not also join us in all of the rigors of the school of hard knocks? Did all the praise and adulation that many gave him diminish his personal agony? All the titles and acclaim did not change his trip to Calvary. "If you are the Son of God," some shouted, "save yourself and come down from the cross and we will believe." When are we going to learn that God just doesn't do things our way? God's ways, as many in the Scriptures have said, are past finding out. I am glad for this, however, because if I could ever begin to figure God out, I might have to question which of us is really God.

God has given us a wonderful example in Jesus as to how we might expect to grow into mature human beings. The next time you begin to cry out, "Why me, Lord?" remember that Jesus too cried out, "Why me, Lord?" As the saying goes, "What's good for the goose is good for the gander." It is a vivid demonstration that God is not partial toward anyone. The Passion narratives that describe the final days before Jesus was placed on the cross were never meant to make us brood or concentrate on the agonies of this portion of his life. As I have said before, we must remember that the incident of the cross in Jesus' life was relatively minor compared to the glory God wants us to see in the experiences of Jesus' life. The fact of the matter is simple: if he didn't die he could not be raised! The Resurrection is the main point; let us not lose sight of that. Let us also remember that death on the cross was probably the crudest way to die at that time in history. If the incident of the cross teaches us anything, it demonstrates that God will be with us even through the worst of times. God demonstrates his promise that he is with us always and will never leave us alone. God did not abandon Jesus, and he will not abandon us. This is the positive and life-giving message of the cross experience. As practical and helpful as this may be, however, we can never lose sight of the fact that total victory was only hours and days away. Easter happened! In every circumstance of pain and suffering, Easter will happen for us also! It may, at times, seem much longer than days or hours, but Easter will come. This is the great promise of the Christian message.

This is what we have and this is what we proclaim: We are a part of a living tradition and we must get on with living. As we move along in life, things change, and the more we move along the more things will change. Change is difficult for many people, but it can never be avoided. To resist change by trying to keep older and wonderful traditions current is to fall into the trap of traditionalism, and traditionalism kills. To move along with change and allow the older traditions to change into new traditions for a new day is the way to life in all its fullness. We do not need to fear this progress, because God is always with us, and God enables us to change. Jesus did not want to die; we do not want to die. God did not want Jesus to end, and God does not want us to end. Death, in fact, is not an end but a process of transition to something new. It may be seen in the birth of a child. The child must "die" in its fetal life so it might come forth from the mother into its new form of life. This process of transition may be short or long, rather easy or filled with pain and struggle, but it must happen. Death is never a punishment to be feared, according to Scripture, but a process to bring us into a more active and on-going life with God. It is never prudent to concentrate on the birthing process, but it is wonderful as we wait with expectation and finally hold this new life in our hands after the process is over.

The Passion of Jesus should never become our focus. We should always live with expectation and focus on the Resurrection. We have the promise that God is always with us in every circumstance, and we have the right to live with the expectation that we will always come forth to new life. During the hard times of life, we learn by experience that this Gospel is true. The best preparation for living is life itself!

One of the incredible gifts which helps us live in our world today is the myriad of stories in Holy Scripture from the earliest times. The Bible is filled with the witness of many people over thousands of years who personally, as individuals and in community experienced the loving kindness of God. They tell us many times that they found God to be a provider, to always be faithful and eternal, because God never abandoned them. Perhaps the reason so many people still connect to reading these stories from the Bible is because they are not dissimilar from their own experience of the divine. People who are aware of the presence of God in their lives sense that they hold something in common with these earlier pilgrims of faith. We are always encouraged when we come into contact with others who may have shared our experiences and vision of life. The Bible, then, is a living book for many of us who are continuing our journey of faith into the future.

When the inspiration of these witnesses is received in an open way as a written record of their journey we are the inheritors of a tremendous gift from them and from God. We must be careful, however, not to memorialize them in the fashion of traditionalism by insisting that God will always act in the same manner as was true in their time. God's time is not our time. God is capable of serving all of us in our own time and according to our own needs. The precepts of the universe are too broad to be confined to such a narrow view with such limited capabilities. The Bible is probably the most abused book when it comes to those who are beset with traditionalism. "Thus saith the Lord" is used mostly to set in place the tradition of a certain time rather than to enable one to understand God's ability to help us acquire a similar or wholly new tradition for our time and need. We must always concentrate on the love and grace of God that was active in their lives rather than the tradition or the solution given to their need.

Our God is not limited by time and space. Just because God solved a particular problem or brought wisdom and strength to the world at one time does not fix for all time the way it will always be done. God may be the same yesterday, today, and forever. The progressive revelation of God in our world has enriched us in magnificent ways through the course of history.

When the biblical record began, humankind did not even know how to write, and inventions were few. For a long time nothing much new happened. After the invention of the printing press and the industrial revolution things began to change more rapidly. As we entered the twentieth century, circumstances began to change rapidly. Now, with the computer and the Internet we can hardly keep up with change. There is so much information available, no one person will be able to see and read it all. The way we live and function today is absolutely and completely different from those who were before us, especially those who lived in biblical times. No way could they have even imagined what life would be like, as we now know it. I am also sure that we cannot now even imagine what life will actually be like in the next century. How then could we expect that God's words spoken in biblical times would be for all time and eternity? We have words and concepts that were not possible for them to hear or understand. Consequently, when we try to use their words and concepts in our life and circumstances today we too become confused and bewildered. You cannot put new wine into old wineskins, as the Scripture tells us.

So we must understand that it is impossible for us to follow in the biblical tradition of their day. Not because those traditions were not excellent for their time, but because we are no longer in their time. To try to use and celebrate these older traditions is to be caught up in traditionalism. Our tradition of faith need not adhere to a set of rules and regulations that were applicable to a former time. Our tradition of faith need not adhere to theological or philosophical precepts that were formulated in a former time. When the Scriptures tell us that the just will live by faith, they do not suggest that there are eternally stated rules, regulations, or time-related precepts that must be followed. The faith Scripture is pointing to is a living relationship with the One who makes it all happen. It is a covenant, marriage, or partnership with God, who invites us to enter such a state. It is a lively and progressive union that, once entered, brings us into a more perfect relationship with our world and others in it. It is an individual and community venture that, like all of life, is constantly changing.

The Scripture uses marriage as an example of such a divine union with God. There are many stories in Scripture that use marriage in such a manner, so let me share my thoughts with you using marriage as well. There are many forms of marriage in our world, and we might say there are no two marriages exactly alike. This is true not only in the ceremony which may begin a marriage, but in the life fulfillment of that marriage.

Since most couples in America usually choose each other, we tend to forget that, in most of the world, families still choose who will marry. How couples are chosen will vary according to the social customs of the area's residents. For the greater part of human history people married within the same clan, religion, and class. It is only recently, with the growing interaction of many societies and the convenience of intercontinental travel, that couples may be very divergent in societal connection. This has led to a dramatic change in the planning, the ceremony, and the expectation of the marriage itself. 1 hope these words are sufficient to bring to your attention the great variety in marriage customs that has always existed around our world, and the probability that changes will continue to develop as societies and customs mingle and merge in the future.

The interesting thing to me, however, is that marriage continues. Even though the traditions of the past are incorporated or replaced by modem traditions, people still marry. Even though a significant number of marriages end in divorce, those individuals tend to get married again. There is an evident human need for people to come together, besides the practical need for the propagation of our species. People have a clear mystical and emotional need to form an interdependence of body, mind, and spirit to build for the future. The need for this bonding is much stronger than the traditions that encourage and enable it to be. The traditions, even as they change, only provide the public awareness and celebration of such a union.

I believe marriage continues to be small picture of a much greater and more important union and relationship with the One who is the primal force of our entire existence. This need for God in our lives is strong and powerful for most people. This need creates a great void in the very heart of our humanity when it is not met and celebrated. It is essential because it clarifies the roots and resources of who we are, it gives vitality and vision as to what we are and can be in the present, and it moves us into the future with hope and confidence for all eternity. This is God's design and desire for us, and it cannot be bound by any tradition, especially when it grows into traditionalism. This relationship cannot be fully- defined by any tradition—past, present, or future. This relationship is created by the traditions people have established in coming together to celebrate this wonderful grace and love, which fills the whole of the universe continually.

I urge you, therefore, to develop a living tradition, a way of living that enables you to express to others the depth and breadth of this wonderful presence among us. One that enables you to become what God has called you to be, not a tradition that forces you to act out what others expect of you. At a time in history when people have more choices in their venue of life than ever before, it seems strange that so many people feel trapped and bound. The stress of conformity is a great burden for most. Even in the United States, which calls itself the land of the free and the home of the brave, too many are overwhelmed by the pressures of modern society. the trend is to bend toward the pressure to conform rather than to be continually transformed by the power of God.

Unfortunately, too many religious communities are geared toward conformity. They are bastions of traditionalism rather than living communities that encourage us to grow and flourish. Organized religion is more often a social structure with rules and regulations to keep us in place rather than a living organization of people who encourage and help us broaden our knowledge, strengthen our souls, and enable us to do and accomplish in life what we would never be able to do alone. Places where God is worshipped, not the traditions of people about God.

I encourage you to find and attend a progressive church, so you may make progress in your life and bring hope to others. Be open to the power of God in your life and enjoy the opportunity of sharing that strength with others. In the name of the living God, may you find life eternal.

Made in the USA
Charleston, SC
12 March 2016